TRY N TO LAUGH CHALLENGE

12 YEAR OLD EDITION

JOKE BOOK

Silly Fun Kid publishing

© copyright 2020 Silly Fun Kid Publishing–All rights reserved

The content contained within this book may not be reproduced, duplicated, or transmitted without direct written permission from the author or publisher

Thank you for choosing Silly Fun Kid

Silly Fun Kid is a nature comedian, represents the work of comedian friends, they try to send some happiness to the little stars and make them laugh and enjoy reading jokes.

Copyright © 2020 Silly Fun Kid The content contained within this book may not be reproduced, duplicated, or transmitted without direct written permission from the author or publisher.

Have a question? please visit
sites.google.com/view/sillyfunkid/books
or
use **QR Code**

to learn more and send us message.

We hope you have a great funny time with this book if you like our books please support us with a review this encourages us to do more things .

Try Not To Laugh Challenge

 ## BONUS PLAY!

Join our Joke Club and get the Bonus play PDF!

   Simply type THIS URL:

https://sites.google.com/view/sillyfunkid/free?authuser=0

Or
use **QR code**

and you will get 20 best Funny jokes!
by Silly Fun Kid

Welcome to the try not laugh challenge

How to play the game?
The try not to laugh challenge is made up of 10 rounds, every round has 2 jesters, each player has a jester, and should make the second player laugh score to the points.
after completing the 10 rounds add all points and find the winner! "Master"

Round 11 : "THE ROUND GIFT"
the round 11 is the rounds gift which is the champion should get a gift!

Who can play this game?
the try not to laugh challenge is a super fun fast easy game for the family or friends to play together and get tons of laughs!

JOKESTER 1   JOKESTER 1

Rules of The Try Laugh Challenge

- bring the player's friends or family members, get your pencil, prepare your comedy power.

- determine who's the "jokester1" and "jokester2"

- jokester 1 will hold the book and read the jokes.

- pass the book to jokester 2 read jokes.

- once the round completed score points.

- the same thing until round 11, then add all points to find the champion!

- all these guides you will find on the bottom the pages after.

- give to the champion any gifts!

Ready! time to play don't laugh

JOKESTER 1

at what time farm animals wakeup? /1
at hen oclock!

what did cat say to the donkey? /1
beautiful smile!

why the turtle can't run fast? /1
because she doesn't care!

what do we call a cow that gives you sour milk? /1
cow end of validity!

 JOKES TOTAL /4

JOKESTER 1

Where did the turkey and his wife go on Friday night?
To the rooster-ant!   /1

Why did the superhero go to the baseball game?
He'd heard that someone had stolen a base!   /1

Why is the broom boring?
All it was doing was collecting dust.   /1

Why don't big hens play in the jungle?
Too many cheetahs!   /1

 **JOKES TOTAL**   /4

pass the book to jokester 2! ➡

JOKESTER 2

Why are the cactuses so
dangerous?   /1
It's full of blades!

Why did the bear break the
 wooden car?   /1
It wooden go!

What's the difference between a
table and a newspaper?   /1
Ever tried swatting a fly with a table?

Where does a geologist go to
Friday night?   /1
Go to a rock concert!

 JOKES TOTAL   /4

JOKESTER 2

What is the name of ugly noodles!
spaghetti!
___/1

What do you call pizza without cheese?
Ketchup!
___/1

What do you call a sleeping bull?
The good night bull!
___/1

How do snails fight?
They release foams!
___/1

 **JOKES TOTAL** ___/4

time to add up your points!

SCORE BOARD

In each jokester's add total jokes points for this round!

JOKESTER 1

_____ /8
TOTAL

JOKESTER 2

_____ /8
TOTAL

_____
ROUND 1 WINNER

JOKESTER 1

Are any fish monsters good at math? /1
No unless you Count shark!

Who helps little ghost cross the road on the way to school? /1
The Crossing transparent!

Why did pumpkin terrible in math?
They pump in the exam! /1

How do we know octopus was married more than once?
Because he wore many rings! /1

 JOKES TOTAL /4

JOKESTER 1

What has four letters and starts with a stinky smell?
fart!   /1

What did a ruler say to a pen deriver
take the straight path!   /1

what did the English pen say to the Chinese pen?
do you have a black belt in karate?   /1

Why did the worker get fired from the lemon juice factory?
he made it sour!   /1

 **JOKES TOTAL**   /4

pass the book to jokester 2! ➡

JOKESTER 2

What do you call a donkey with prise?
A wonkey!   /1

why did the turle lazy?
because she's never mind!   /1

what did the pen say to the notebook?
let's take a stroll in a write!   /1

Why did the math book say to the kid?
can you help me to solve my problem!   /1

 JOKES TOTAL   /4

JOKESTER 2

Why you can't play with monsters?
Why you can't play with monsters? /1

abracadabra stooop farting!!
abracadabra stooop farting!! /1

Why is spaghetti called spaghetti?
Because they're not wearing any clothes! /1

What kind of books do old cows like to read? /1
no, he likes to read moos-paper!

 **JOKES TOTAL** /4

time to add up your points!

SCORE BOARD

In each jokester's add total jokes points for this round!

JOKESTER 1

———— /8
TOTAL

JOKESTER 2

———— /8
TOTAL

————
ROUND 1 WINNER

JOKESTER 1

What did the clock do when it was eating ice cream?
It went back four seconds!   /1

What's where does the arrogant cow go in the evening?
to play a pool table!   /1

Which hand is better for chopping onions?
anyway you will cry!   /1

I ordered a turkey and an egg online.
I'll let you know!   /1

 JOKES TOTAL   /4

JOKESTER 1

What did husband pizza say to his wife when she put on a lot of makeup?   /1
ooh! you look like a witch looking for cheese!

What do you call a man who say always no?   /1
noman!

Why did the cow cross the road?   /1
she wanted to lose a little weight!

Why ghosts can't drive?
Because they don't have driving license!   /1

 **JOKES TOTAL**   /4

pass the book to jokester 2! ➡

JOKESTER 2

What kind of ghosts like to go bowling? /1
scary ghosts!

What kind of cake can fly? /1
A plain cake!

why did chicken make a website?
he wanted to sell some eggs online! /1

What happened to the gorilla who refused to sleep?
He was charged with resisting a rest! /1

 **JOKES TOTAL** /4

JOKESTER 2

Where do sheep go when they broke?
To the retail store! ___/1___

Do police always snore?
No, only when they're asleep! ___/1___

What's the worse mom joke ever?
This one! ___/1___

What job does the belt hate?
carry pants! ___/1___

 **JOKES TOTAL** ___/4___

time to add up your points!

SCORE BOARD

In each jokester's add total jokes points for this round!

JOKESTER 1

/8
———
TOTAL

JOKESTER 2

/8
———
TOTAL

———————
ROUND 1 WINNER

JOKESTER 1

How do you make eleven an even number?
Take away the 'el'!   /1

How many pears grow on a tree?
All of them!   /1

What do you call a panda with no teeth?
All of them!   /1

What's the difference between a dog and a cat?
cats fart too much!   /1

 JOKES TOTAL   /4

JOKESTER 1

What is the bull's favorite sport?
wrestling! ___/1

What happened when the dragon sneezes the bank?
nothing, he just burned all money! ___/1

Why did snail faint?
because the elephant fart it and he can't run! ___/1

What do ants use to call each other?
Cell phones! ___/1

 **JOKES TOTAL** ___/4

pass the book to jokester 2! ➡

JOKESTER 2

What does the toilet use to write?
toilet paper!   /1

Did you hear about the lion who escaped from the park?
Don't worry, he is behind us!   /1

What do you call a puppy with no legs?
You can call him whatever you like but   /1
he's not coming!

What do you call a crocodile with no legs and arms?   /1
A green thing!

 JOKES TOTAL   /4

JOKESTER 2

Why do you go to school every day?
Because your school won't come to you!   /1

What's red, juicy, and lemon his uncle?
An orange disguised as a strawberry!   /1

What's the same with a spider and a ladybug?
They're both insects, except the spider working hard!   /1

              /1

What do you call a melon?
an egg has not lost weight!

JOKES TOTAL   /4

time to add up your points! ➡

SCORE BOARD

In each jokester's add total jokes points for this round!

JOKESTER 1

_____ /8
TOTAL

JOKESTER 2

_____ /8
TOTAL

_____
ROUND 1 WINNER

JOKESTER 1

Why did cats wear yellow socks?
So they can hide upside-down on the birthday cake!   /1

What's green and looks like an apple?
an apple!   /1

What do you call a frog make crumpets?
A crumpet frog!   /1

what favorite thing do ghost like to do at the weekend?
watching a scary movie!   /1

 **JOKES TOTAL**   /4

JOKESTER 1

Why did the shark go to the dentist?
he ate so much fish candy!   /1

What happens if schools closed?
nothing, you will study online!   /1

What do you call a cow that knows karate?
A beef chop!   /1

What did the pig say when he arrived from the gym?
I have to take a mud shower!   /1

 **JOKES TOTAL**   /4

pass the book to jokester 2! ➡

JOKESTER 2

What is blue and has green wheels? /1

sea .....I lied about the wheels!

Why are turtles slow? /1
Because they're carrying their house on their back!

Why didn't the tennis player eat dinner? /1
he couldn't use his hands! he couldn't use his hands!

What's a rat's favorite dessert? /1
cheese-cream!

 **JOKES TOTAL** /4

JOKESTER 2

What do you call a zombie who's really loud? /1
Mike!

What's a shark's favorite food?
fish bubbles! /1

what happened when the elephant rode the swing?
nothing, the swing left life!! /1

how do you know that gorilla got a fight? /1
you will find teeth in the ground, they like boxing!

JOKES TOTAL /4

time to add up your points! ➡

SCORE BOARD

In each jokester's add total jokes points for this round!

JOKESTER 1

/8
———
TOTAL

JOKESTER 2

/8
———
TOTAL

———————
ROUND 1 WINNER

JOKESTER 1

What do you do if you find a big bee in your room?
I will ask her if she's the queen, the queen can't hurt

/1

What do you call two crocodiles on the floor?
shoes!

/1

What is a mermaids dream?
to have legs to go shopping on Black Friday!

/1

Why did the penguin win a prize?
Because he drew a fish with no teeth!

/1

JOKES TOTAL /4

JOKESTER 1

Why don't you ever see an ostrich in primary school?
Because they're all in high school!   /1

Where would you find a chicken?
The same place where she lay eggs!   /1

What's black and can't climb trees?
A TV!   /1

Why do dogs like walking?
Because they can't fly!   /1

JOKES TOTAL   /4

pass the book to jokester 2! ➡

JOKESTER 2

how do birds know can fly?
They believe can fly!   /1

Why do cheetahs always win the game?   /1
Because they always cheat!

Why did the horse lose the race?
he got diarrhea in a run!   /1

Why are ghosts very good at math?   /1
Because they can see the solution!

 JOKES TOTAL   /4

JOKESTER 2

how do you know cats and dogs got into fights?
they will look like zombies!   /1

why did the witch kick the broom?
she didn't clean the house!   /1

Which side of a donkey has the most hair?
The outside!   /1

What did one frog say to his friend?
Should we walk or catch a fly?   /1

   JOKES TOTAL   /4

time to add up your points!

SCORE BOARD

In each jokester's add total jokes points for this round!

JOKESTER 1

_____ /8
TOTAL

JOKESTER 2

_____ /8
TOTAL

_____
ROUND 1 WINNER

JOKESTER 1

Why did the donkey go to school?
Because he wanted to be a zebra!   /1

What do you call a sleeping dragon?
A fire-snore!   /1

if crocodiles make shoes what frogs make?
slippers!   /1

what do hamburgers like to play at the weekend?
play meat-ball   /1

 JOKES TOTAL   /4

JOKESTER 1

why didn't the snowman go to school?
he cath a cold!   /1

where did mosquitos go on 31 December?
to annoying the revelers at the new year party   /1

what is a melon dream?
to become watermelon!   /1

what did ghosts buy online?
some transparence clothes!   /1

 JOKES TOTAL   /4

pass the book to jokester 2! ➡

JOKESTER 2

what is the bet the bunny won?
24 carrots!
/1

how do you fix pizza had an accident?
with tomato paste
/1

What do you call turtle sleeping on it's back?
Yuga turtle!
/1

What do you call taller hose?
Giraffe horse!
/1

 **JOKES TOTAL** /4

JOKESTER 2

What did math book say to other books? ___/1

I have many problems!

What do you call pizza without cheese? ___/1

Ketchup!

What do you call a sleeping bull?

The good night bull! ___/1

what did the cheese say to tomato sauce? ___/1

sauce to meet you!

 **JOKES TOTAL** ___/4

time to add up your points! ➡

SCORE BOARD

In each jokester's add total jokes points for this round!

JOKESTER 1   /8
                ———————
                 TOTAL

JOKESTER 2   /8
                ———————
                 TOTAL

————————————
ROUND 1 WINNER

JOKESTER 1

where was the mushroom invited?
to the pizza party!   /1

what type of person dragon doesn't like?
fireman!   /1

what is the difference between an elephant fan and a baby?
a baby will stop whining after awhile!   /1

what does Aligator pack for camping trips?
the crocodile necessities!   /1

 JOKES TOTAL   /4

JOKESTER 1

what do you need for a birthday in the jungle?
a cake gorilla and a candle fly! ___/1

why does panda like old tv?
because they're black and white! ___/1

why does koala an introvert?
he wanted to be a bear! ___/1

why did the flies take to prison?
they drove a garbage truck with no license drive ___/1

 **JOKES TOTAL** ___/4

pass the book to jokester 2! ➡

JOKESTER 2

why don't turtles like fast food?
because they can't catch it!   /1

What do chimpanzees need in the sea?
Swimwear!   /1

what do you do if you find a panda in your toilet?
let it finish   /1

what did the goat say when the soccer team lost?
mehhh! come on!   /1

 JOKES TOTAL   /4

JOKESTER 2

what do you call a sheep likes cleaning?
room-baa! /1

why is hard to have a conversation with a bee?
they always buzz in! (butt in) /1

what did the bear say when he finds three places to fish?
fish! fish! fish! wow /1

how do you prepare for the exam? /1
I equip all the weapons to launch an attack!

JOKES TOTAL /4

time to add up your points!

SCORE BOARD

In each jokester's add total jokes points for this round!

JOKESTER 1   /8

TOTAL

JOKESTER 2   /8

TOTAL

_____

ROUND 1 WINNER

JOKESTER 1

where do goats like to travel?
to chica-goat!   /1

what did giraffes say to the waiter?
I want two tall hamburguer!   /1

why should you not write a book on spider?
because writing book on papper is much easier!   /1

how do zombies know when ther's somthing wrong?
it smells a bit rotten!   /1

 JOKES TOTAL   /4

JOKESTER 1

how do a group of mosquitos make a decision?
throw a coin! ____/1

why don't ants fly?
because they're not big enough to be pilots ____/1

what kind of shoes do penguins like to wear?
ice shoes! ____/1

what do ghosts like to eat in candy shope?
I scream! ____/1

 **JOKES TOTAL** ____/4

pass the book to jokester 2! ➡

JOKESTER 2

why didn't dinosaur go to school?
he was still dino-snoring!   /1

what do judge put in theurdrinks?
just ice!   /1

what he wanted octopus tobecome in the future?
an octocoper!   /1

way was spider dangerous?
he was well armed!   /1

 **JOKES TOTAL**   /4

JOKESTER 2

why did cockroachs get in trubble?   /1

they went out to celebrate in the kitchen and the old witch saw them!

why do gorilla hate tests?   /1

because they get stumped by the questions!

how do owls get on the internet?   /1

they log in!

what did the cow cook for its neighbor the pig?   /1

dung cake!

JOKES TOTAL   /4

time to add up your points!

SCORE BOARD

In each jokester's add total jokes points for this round!

JOKESTER 1

/8
___
TOTAL

JOKESTER 2

/8
___
TOTAL

___
ROUND 1 WINNER

JOKESTER 1

what did pizza say when she looked
in the mirror?   /1
halloume!

how do mouses take selfie?
they say "cheese"!   /1

what was the snoman searching at
in the refrigator?
his carrot!   /1

why don't you ever see ghosts
wear shoes?
because they have a great measure!   /1

 JOKES TOTAL   /4

JOKESTER 1

what do you call a doctor who never farts in public?
private tutor!   /1

two cows are in a tractor, one says to other...
do you know how to drive this thing?   /1

why are giraffes, good dancers?
they have a long neck!   /1

what did the dentist say to the pirates?
are those teeth or marine rocks!   /1

 **JOKES TOTAL**   /4

pass the book to jokester 2! ➡

JOKESTER 2

Why did the skeleton make a crazy party?
Because there nobody at home!

___/1

Why did the witch put her money in the freezer?
She wanted cold hard cash!

___/1

What do you give a sick zombie?
nothing, he rotten!

___/1

What is the most expensive food?
A goldfish grilled!

___/1

 **JOKES TOTAL** ___/4

JOKESTER 2

what do you call a dragon fart?
a blast from myths!   /1

why did the chef cry on TV?
no, he peeled the onions!
                                   /1

Why were ghosts screaming?
she was watching a scary movie!
                                   /1

why were strawberries sad?   /1
it was in the jam!

 **JOKES TOTAL**   /4

time to add up your points!

SCORE BOARD

In each jokester's add total jokes points for this round!

JOKESTER 1

_____ /8

TOTAL

JOKESTER 2

_____ /8

TOTAL

_____

ROUND 1 WINNER

ROUND

11

ROUND GIFT

JOKESTER 1

what did the chicken say to the waiter?
put me in the bill!   /1

what did one fish say to the other fish when they were watching a movie?
stooop farting bubbles!!!   /1

What does starling birds do in the winter?
traveling for vacation then will be back in the spring   /1

what did the snowman say to the dragon?
don't laugh, you will make me water!!   /1

JOKES TOTAL   /4

JOKESTER 1

where did cows go on a Friday night?
to play the moo-moo fart challenge!   /1

how do you stop the baby from craying?
put some a boring song!   /1

why did the eggs break all in the movie?
he attended a comedy-hen movie!   /1

why didn't the dentist extract the patient's tooth?
no, he just had diarrhea!   /1

 **JOKES TOTAL**   /4

pass the book to jokester 2! ➡

JOKESTER 2

What kind of exam does a cow give his students?   /1
A dung test!

What's did pen say to other pens in the castle?   /1
The ruler is coming!

What part of a sheep weighs the most?   /1
The meat!

What did the elephant say when he saw his self in the mirror?   /1
I look like a fat mammoth!

 **JOKES TOTAL**   /4

JOKESTER 2

What did math book say to other books?   /1

I have many problems!

why did the pirate boat sinking in the sea?   /1

they didn't agree on the direction!

where did 12 candles go in the night?   /1

to celebrate the kid's birthday party!

what is the chimpanzees' favorite game?   /1

telling farting jokes!

JOKES TOTAL   /4

time to add up your points! ➡

SCORE BOARD

In each jokester's add total jokes points for this round!

JOKESTER 1

___/8
TOTAL

JOKESTER 2

___/8
TOTAL

_____
ROUND 1 WINNER

FINAL SCORE BOARD

	jokester 1 /8	jokester 2 /8
Round 1		
Round 2		
Round 3		
Round 4		
Round 5		
Round 6		
Round 7		
Round 8		
Round 9		
Round 10		
Round 11		
Total		

THE CHAMPION IS:

_____

Congradulation!

CHEK OUT OUR

Visit our Amazon store at:

OTHER JOKE BOOKS!

www.Amazon.com/author/sillyfunkid

Printed in Great Britain
by Amazon

33050277R00046